Regulated Learners
in
Minutes a Day

Brain-Body Activities
for Ventral Learning

Dr. Debra Em Wilson

Integrated Learner Press

Integrated Learner Press
12112 N. Rancho Vistoso Blvd.
Suite A150, PO Box 142
Oro Valley, AZ 85737

Canva and Pixabay images used for cover design and internal graphics.
Drawings and graphic design by Linda McGinnis and Kathy Martens

Dear Reader,

I've experienced the heartache of having a child born with a constellation of genetic and developmental challenges. When I was looking for answers, the internet was in its infancy and nothing like it is today. I had to search hard for answers both as a mom and a reading specialist in the public schools. At home, my daughter wasn't making progress. I was told by doctors in various ways that she'd, "never walk,talk, or function in a meaningful way." My reading students weren't making much progress either!

My search led me to the ultimate solution for my daughter's growth and my students' success. I had to provide opportunities to wire the brain through the body, creating new neural networks using embodied cognition (learning with the body). Today there is a large body of science supporting using rhythmic, patterned movement to improve learning, focus, and regulation. This type of movement also reduces the impact of trauma on the mind-body system.

I introduce the concept of *ventral learning* in my book *The Polyvagal Path to Joyful Learning*. Ventral learning means to be in a learning state that includes being curious, motivated, regulated, and resilient. To be a ventral learner, the mind and body must work together and support one another. What you do to one, you do to the other. A more organized, regulated body leads to a more organized, regulated brain. These activities are designed to wire the brain-body system for optimized learning.

Thanks for all you do for children every day. I love hearing from you. You can reach me at info@schoolmoves.com. Consider taking a course if you haven't already. We dive deep into these activities and the science behind them.

Warmly,

Debra Em

Table of Contents

LET'S BEGIN!

QUICK TIPS

1. The Let's Begin! activities are foundational moves that can be used any time when needed throughout the day. You'll see these moves repeated in the Monday Minute Moves section where they are integrated into quick routines to support focus and regulation.

2. As soon as students know the moves, begin adding academics to the moves. Students count, skip count, recite multiplication facts, spell, recite word families, and so on. Remember, the body learns 10 times faster than the brain and forgets 10 times slower. If you want to learn something faster, use embodied cognition (involve the body).

3. To improve interoception, ask students how their hands feel while doing dots and squeezies or how their legs feel when doing cross crawls. Ask if they feel any change inside like less stress or more stress. Sometimes doing these moves can create more stress if a student has motor planning or sensory issues. Watch for signs of stress and ask support staff for help if needed.

4. Always proceed with safety and connection in mind. Students need to feel a sense of safety and connection with one another when they learn and do these moves.

5. Adding music is a fun way to do the moves. After any upbeat activity, do the Minute Moves for Calming routine in the next section.

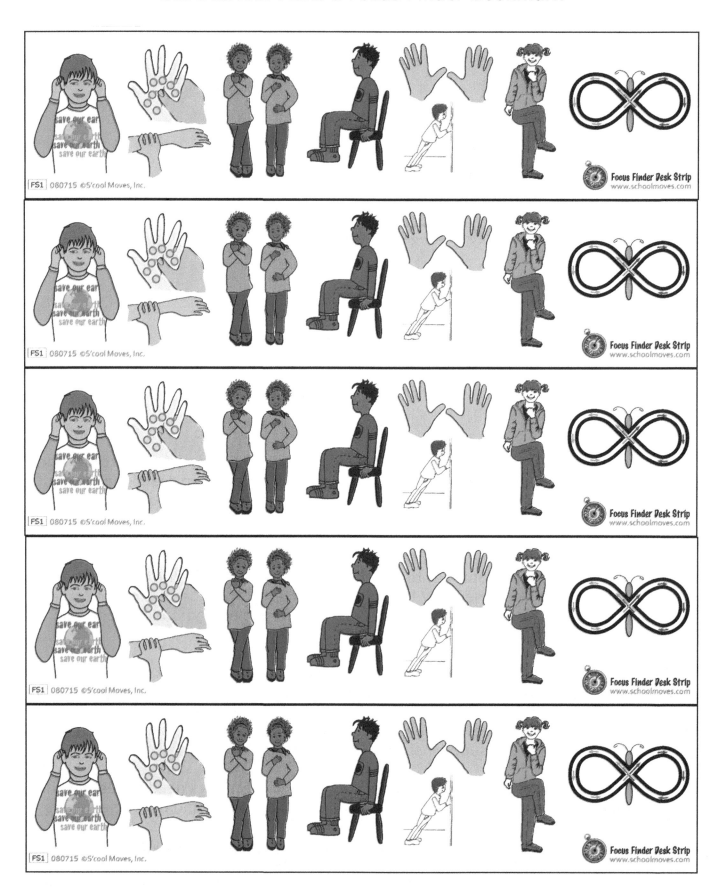

Directions for Teaching the Moves on the Focus Finder Bookmark

The Focus Finder Desk Strip was created because teachers needed a way to quickly provide focus strategies for students without interrupting their instruction time.

Teach all the moves on the strip in advance and let students practice the moves until they are familiar and comfortable with each one. Then, during the day, simply point to the movement a student needs without verbalizing instructions. The student does the movement independently, usually in sets of ten (ten Dots, ten Squeezies, etc.).

Encourage independence by repeating daily something like this, "When you need to refocus, calm down, wake up, or get ready for a test, this Focus Strip reminds you of the different ways you can be your best learner." Ultimately, students should no longer need prompting and take responsibility for doing the move they need on their own.

The Focus Finder activities can be alerting or calming depending on the child's unique sensory system. In general, Dots & Squeezies, Wall Push-ups, and Chair Lifts are quieting to the system. The Figure 8 is integrating and great to use prior to testing or new learning situations. Cross Crawls awaken and integrate when students stand and do ten at first signs of yawning or learning fatigue. Listening Ears work well for talkative children who need to refocus or can be used proactively for a group who needs to listen to instructions.

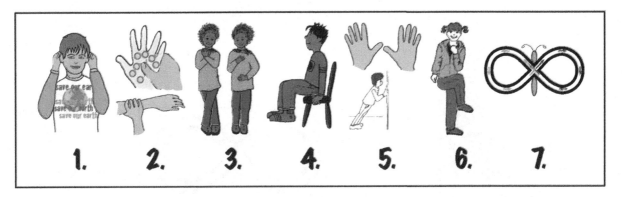

1. **Listening Ears:** Massage and unroll the ears gently. Begin at the top of the ears and massage to the bottom of the ears. Repeat five times.

2. **Dots & Squeezies:** Press thumb firmly into and around palm of the hand for a count of ten. Pause and take three deep breaths. Change hands and repeat on other hand.

3. **Pretzels & Heart to Home:** (Pretzels): Cross wrists. Interlock fingers in front of chest. Roll crossed hands under and into chest with thumbs leading while pointed at the floor. Relax shoulders. Cross legs. Tongue is placed at the roof of the mouth. (Heart to Home): Place one hand over the heart, the other hand on the belly. Take three deep breaths. Come to a quiet, focused place in the body.

4. **Chair Lifts:** Lift total weight off chair. Feet are off the floor. Hold for three to five seconds. If too difficult, bring knees to chest without lifting body off chair. Repeat five times.

5. **Wall Push-ups:** Push against the wall. Elbows are bent and tucked in; hands are at chest height. Legs are extended back. Feet are flat on floor.

Modified Chair Lift

6. **Cross Crawls:** While standing, bring opposite knee to elbow, then switch. Repeat ten times.

7. **Butterfly 8's:** On a piece of paper or using a Butterfly 8 card, trace the Figure 8 ten times with the right hand, left hand, and then both hands. Follow with the eyes. Try not to move the head. Keep 8 at midline of body.

Quick Reference Chart to Minute Moves Activities

Calming Moves

Dots & Squeezies or 10/7s

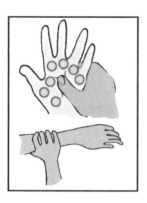

Pretzels & Heart to Home

Listening Ears

Focusing Moves

Chair Lifts

Butterfly 8s

Wall Push-ups

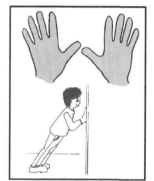

Yawn Buster Moves

Cross Crawls

Mirror Me Moves

Rhythm Tapping

Why these Neurodevelopmental Moves Work

Calming Moves

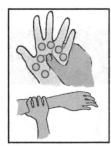

Dots & Squeezies or 10/7s
Deep pressure sends messages from the joints, muscles, and tendons to the brain helping children know where they are in space while also quieting the nervous system.

Listening Ears
Massaging the ears calls attention to the auditory system. Many acupressure points are located on the earlobes so this activity also helps with general well being.

Pretzels & Heart to Home
These moves make the two hemispheres of the brain talk with one another. Each hemisphere has a unique processing style. Both hemispheres talking to one another is needed to learn with ease. Tongue at the roof of the mouth is an emotional regulating technique focusing on the amygdala (emotional center of the brain) and used in cognitive therapy.

Focusing Moves

Chair Lifts
Having strong postural stability creates more availability of energy for academics because the mind and body are working as a team. Weak posture is linked to reduced retenion of academic information.

Butterfly 8s
Figure 8s integrate the visual system so the eyes can work as a team and increase communication between the two hemispheres of the brain.

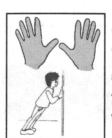

Wall Push-ups
This heavy work activity is the best way to increase focus by sending messages from joints, muscles, and tendons to the brain. When the heel is down, the tendon guard reflex is integrated reducing the fight/flight response. Shoulders, fingers, and posture are also strengthened for writing and sitting upright at the desk.

Yawn Buster Moves

Cross Crawls
Standing gets 30% more blood flow to the brain which increases alertness levels. This cross lateral movement increases the communication between the two hemispheres of the brain and helps improve motor planning.

Mirror Me Moves
This activity activates mirror neurons in the brain and helps with co-regulation with others while also improving motor patterns, sequencing, and organizing the mind-body system.

Rhythm Tapping
The firm tapping on the body increases alertness levels by sending messages from the body to the brain.

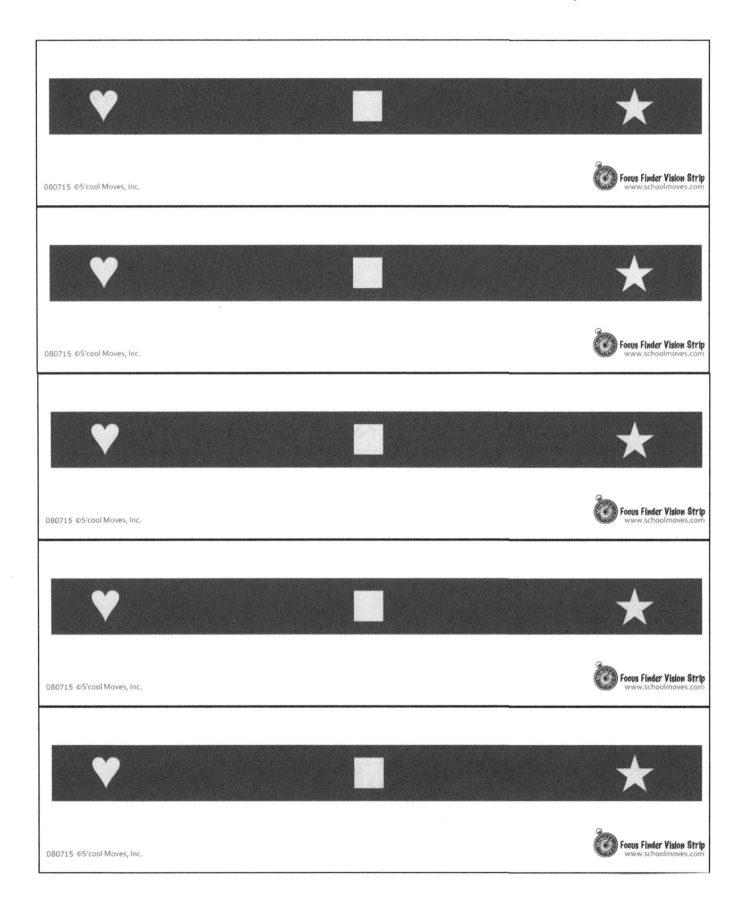

Hold **vision side** of the **Focus Finder Desk Strip** at chest level with elbows bent. Move only the eyes during the warm-up activities. The head should remain still at all times.

Activity #1 Vestibular Warm-ups

Turn head slowly to the right and left while counting to ten.

Tilt head slowly backward and forward while counting to ten.

Tilt head slowly to the right and left while counting to ten.

Activity 2. Fixations
Hold the vision strip while the teacher says, "Look at the square." "Look at the star." "Look at the heart." Mix it up and focus on different symbols. Children take turns leading the activity. Repeat "Look at Me" activity for one minute.

 look at ■, look at ★, look at ♥, 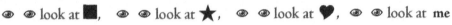 look at **me**

Activity 3. Saccades
Move eyes quickly between two symbols. "Look at the star." "Look at the heart." Move eyes back and forth between the symbols like in the tic-toc action of a clock. Eyes move quickly left to right and right to left. Repeat "Tic Tocs" for 30 seconds.

→★, ♥←, →★, ♥←

Activity 4. Convergence
Hold vision strip, arms out straight, and look at one shape. Keep looking at the shape while slowing bringing strip in toward nose. The strip should come in about one inch from the nose. Repeat "Eye Push-ups" five times.

Activity 5. Near to Far Focus
Look at a shape on the vision strip with arms bent so the strip is at reading distance from the eyes. Next, look at an object on the wall directly ahead. Repeat looking near and far five times.

Look near

Look far

MONDAY
MINUTE MOVES

QUICK TIPS

1. A big part of S'cool Moves is student ownership of their moves so they can become active operators of their learning and behavior systems. When students lead the routines, there's more engagement. As soon as students know the routines, implement leadership roles. Each routine has a job card to go with it. Add jobs to your daily schedule. When students see their names next to one of the Minute Moves jobs, they take it seriously and hone their leadership skills.

2. By teaching students to lead the routines, they can do them when there's a substitute. I've heard so many stories of students leading with substitutes and impressing them to no end. When the class becomes dysregulated, the leader says, "I'm the focus leader. I think we need to do our focus routine."

3. During the Core Out the Door activity, note that postural stability impacts reading comprehension. The brain has a difficult time remembering things when it has to focus on sitting upright.

4. The fine motor routine does much more than work on writing skills. Moving the hand is empirically proven to improve learning and memory. Gesturing is one of the most powerful ways to reduce cognitive load.

5. Consider creating a push place where students can go to do heavy work while reading or spelling words.

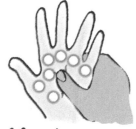

Step 1. Dots

Press thumb firmly into and around palm of the hand for a count of ten. Breathe deeply. Change hands. Add academics by counting or spelling.

Step 2. Squeezies

Squeeze up forearms, upper arms, and shoulders firmly. Breathe deeply. Change to other arm. For older students, refer to Dots and Squeezies as 10/7's. Students do ten deep pressure pushes to the palms and seven squeezes up the arms. For older students, say, "We push and press to reduce the stress."

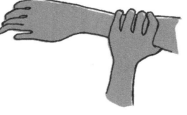

Step 3. Pretzels

Interlock fingers in front of chest. Relax shoulders. Cross legs. Tongue is placed at the roof of the mouth.

Step 4. ♥2 🏠 (Heart to Home)

Place one hand over the heart, the other hand on the belly. Take five deep breaths. Come to a quiet, focused place in the body.

(If students were standing for steps 1-4, begin step 5 upon sitting.)

Step 5. Listening Ears

Massage and unroll the ears gently, beginning at the top of the ears and massaging to the bottom of the ears. Repeat five times.

Use **Focus Finder Desk Strips** to encourage independent self-regulation.

10/7's inspired by Steve Piluso, APE

Give them a job to do.
Calming Consultant
MINUTE MOVES JOB CARDS

www.schoolmoves.com

 JOB CARDS

Minute Moves for Calming

BRAIN WIZARD TEACHABLE MINUTE

Question: Is S'cool Moves just for kids or do adults use these activities, too?

Answer: Athletes naturally do many of the S'cool Moves activities. For instance, a famous American wrestler surprised everyone by winning the Olympics. He said that he had a hard time learning in school, but wrestling made learning easier for him. When he wrestled, he got lots of deep pressure like Dots & Squeezies (10/7's). This helped his brain focus for learning.

www.schoolmoves.com

Job: CALMING CONSULTANT
Goes with Minute Moves for Calming Poster

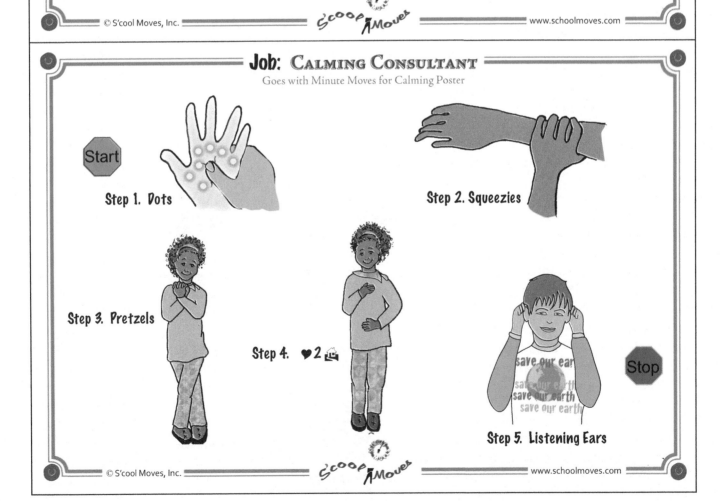

Start

Step 1. Dots

Step 2. Squeezies

Step 3. Pretzels

Step 4. ♥2🏠

Step 5. Listening Ears

Stop

www.schoolmoves.com

Follow the sequence as shown. Perform each movement ten times.

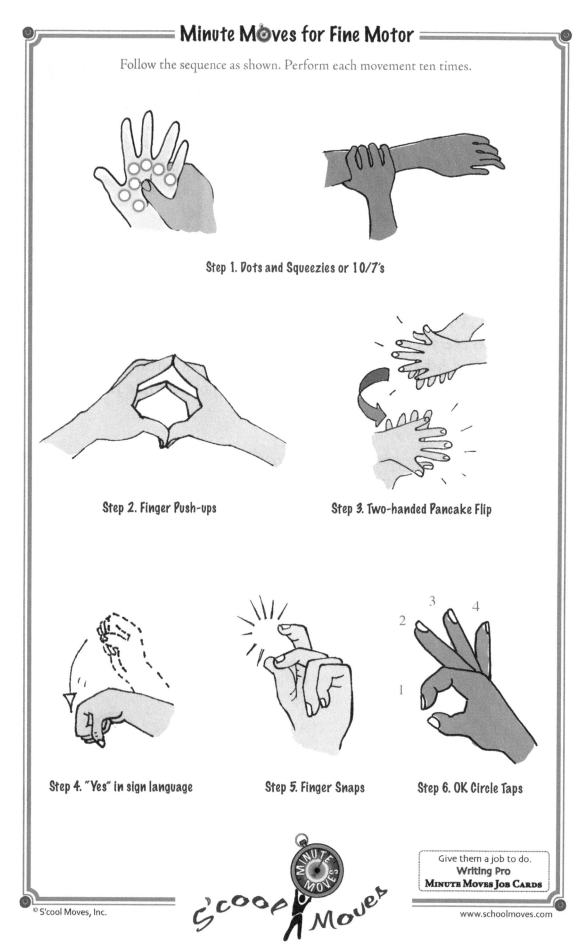

Step 1. Dots and Squeezies or 10/7's

Step 2. Finger Push-ups

Step 3. Two-handed Pancake Flip

Step 4. "Yes" in sign language

Step 5. Finger Snaps

Step 6. OK Circle Taps

Give them a job to do.
Writing Pro
MINUTE MOVES JOB CARDS

S'cool Moves

www.schoolmoves.com

 JOB CARDS

Minute Moves for Fine Motor

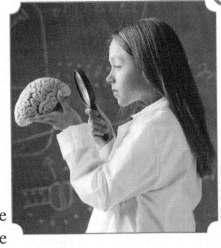

BRAIN WIZARD TEACHABLE MINUTE

Question: How big is my brain?

Answer: If you put your fists together, that is the approximate size of your brain. It weighs about three pounds. Your brain will keep making new connections as long as you keep moving. The fine motor routine warms up your fingers and also helps you think better for writing. The motor cortex in the brain is right next to the frontal lobes. The deep pressure makes the muscles and joints in the body talk to the brain. This creates more connections to help you write better.

© S'cool Moves, Inc.   www.schoolmoves.com

Job: WRITING PRO

Goes with Minute Moves for Fine Motor Poster

Start

Step 1. Dots and Squeezies or 10/7's

Step 2. Finger Push-ups

Step 3. Two-handed Pancake Flip

Step 4. "Yes" in sign language

Step 5. Finger Snaps

Step 6. OK Circle Taps

Stop

© S'cool Moves, Inc.   www.schoolmoves.com

Minute Moves for Writing Posture: Core Out the Door

Strengthen core posture muscles to create a strong, stable base for writing and reading, while also increasing the energy available for executive functioning.

Power Sit and Twist

Sit toward edge of chair, with a straight back and feet flat on the floor. Arms are up, elbows bent, hands at base of skull behind head.

Raise right knee while twisting and lowering left elbow toward the right knee. Now switch and do the other side. Repeat, alternating sides ten times each.

For added difficulty, keep both feet off the ground.

Chair Push-ups

Sit toward edge of chair, with a straight back and feet flat on the floor. Holding on to the edges of the chair, raise the entire body up off the seat, keeping the knees bent. Hold for three to five seconds. Do this ten times.

If this is too challenging, build strength by keeping the bottom on the chair and raising the knees only.

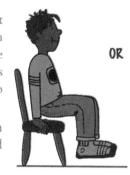 OR

Window Wipers

Sit toward edge of chair, with a straight back and feet flat on the floor. Arms are up, elbows bent, with hands at base of skull behind head. Inhale. Slowly bend upper body to the right as breath is slowly exhaled. Inhale back up to center. Now inhale and do the same thing to the left. Repeat, alternating sides ten times each.

Clark Core Challenge

  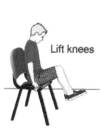 

Lift knees

Sit toward edge of chair, with a straight back, feet flat on the floor, and arms hanging down at sides. Stand up slowly without using arms to help, eyes looking ahead. Grasp chair first, then sit down again slowly. Keeping the bottom on the chair, raise the knees only; bringing chin to chest, eyes looking down. Repeat ten times.

Sit and stand movement inspired by Becky Clark.

Give them a job to do.
Core Coach
MINUTE MOVES JOB CARDS

www.schoolmoves.com

 JOB CARDS

Minute Moves for Writing Posture: Core Out the Door

BRAIN WIZARD TEACHABLE MINUTE

Question: Why should we do our seated core activities at the end of every day?

Answer: When your core muscles are strong, your connections in your brain are strong too. Some children sit on exercise balls while doing their work. Be sure your feet touch the ground when sitting on an exercise ball so you can keep your balance and stay safe. When taking a test or learning a lot of new information, it is best to sit in a chair with your feet on the floor while sitting up tall. This helps you have lots of brain power for learning.

Scoop Moves   www.schoolmoves.com

Job: CORE COACH

Goes with Minute Moves for Writing Posture - Core Out the Door Poster

Start   **Power Sit and Twist**   **Window Wipers**

Clark Core Challenge

Lift legs

Stop

Scoop Moves   www.schoolmoves.com

Step 1. Wall Push-ups

While lined up against a wall, have students perform Wall Push-ups to the count of twenty. If no wall is available, proceed to step 2.

Step 2. Pretzel or Cross Crawl

Students walk with their hands in the Pretzel position or walk while doing Cross Crawls. Before entering the classroom, say: "We are now transitioning from outdoor energy to indoor energy."

Step 3. Transition Cue

Turn off lights in the room, and reinforce: "We are now transitioning from outdoor energy to indoor, quiet energy; please get ready to learn."

Step 4. Dots and Squeezies or 10/7's

To prepare for academics, students do Dots and Squeezies (10/7's) either standing behind their chairs or while sitting.

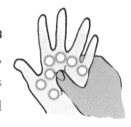 

Step 5. Listening Ears or Butterfly 8 Desk Cards

Students sit down and do Listening Ears or Butterfly 8 desk cards. Say: "I am going to turn on the lights now. We are ready to focus and begin our indoor activities."

Butterfly 8's

Give them a job to do.
Recess Transition Team
MINUTE MOVES JOB CARDS

www.schoolmoves.com

 **Job Cards**

Minute Moves for Recess Refocusing

Brain Wizard Teachable Minute

Question: Why is it important for me to be physically active?

Answer: When you exercise your body, your brain gets a workout too. Your brain needs to stay fit. When the body is healthy, so is the brain. Exercise makes the cells in your brain communicate with each other. This makes it easier for you to learn new things too! It's important to organize all that new energy, so that is why we do the refocusing routine after recess. Be sure to get lots of activity and eat healthy foods. Your brain will thank you for it!

Scoop Moves   www.schoolmoves.com

Job: RECESS TRANSITION TEAM

Goes with Minute Moves for Recess Refocusing Poster

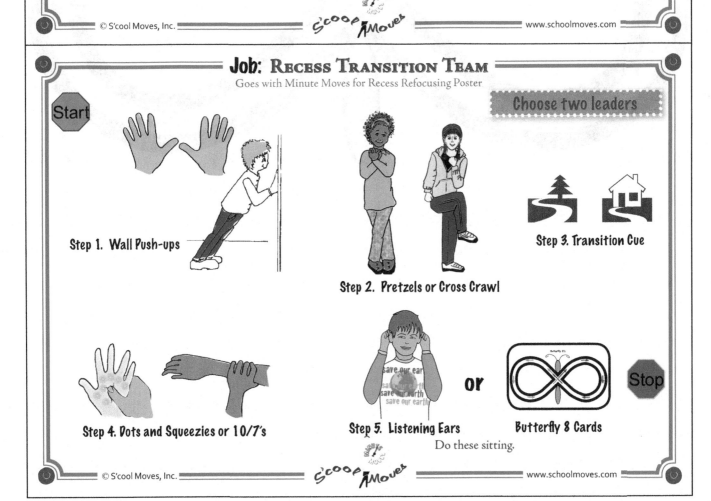

Start

Choose two leaders

Step 1. Wall Push-ups

Step 2. Pretzels or Cross Crawl

Step 3. Transition Cue

Step 4. Dots and Squeezies or 10/7's

Step 5. Listening Ears
Do these sitting.

or

Butterfly 8 Cards

Stop

Scoop Moves   www.schoolmoves.com

Trace in the direction of the arrows ten times with your right hand, left hand, and both hands. Follow with your eyes, try not to move your head. Keep card at midline of body.

Start

Choose one or more activities.

Post spelling words on a wall at eye level.

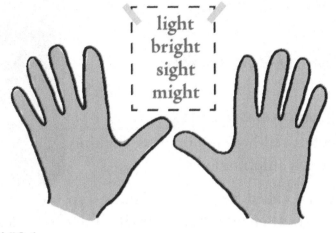

light
bright
sight
might

Wall Push-ups

Push against the wall. Elbows bent and tucked in.

Legs extended back. Feet flat on floor as in diagram.

Practice spelling each letter of a word per each Wall Push-up.

Chair Lift

Lift total weight off chair. Feet are off the floor. Hold for three to five seconds. If too difficult, bring knees to chest without lifting body off chair. While doing chair lifts, have students count by ones, fives, or tens.

Modified Chair Lift

Mirror Me Moves

Students follow a leader who is in front of the class. With slow music playing, the leader slowly moves arms and legs toward midline, away from midline, crossing midline, and in Figure 8 patterns. There is no script. This is a time for creativity and trying out new moves originated by the students. The other students follow along for thirty seconds and then they choose a new leader to come up and lead.

Use **Focus Finder Desk Strips** to encourage independent self-regulation.

Give them a job to do.
Focus Leader
Minute Moves Job Cards

www.schoolmoves.com

 Job Cards

Minute Moves for Focus

BRAIN WIZARD TEACHABLE MINUTE

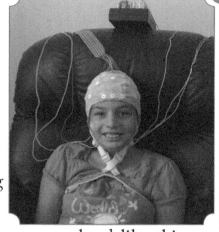

Question: Can doctors tell how my brain is working when I am learning new information?

Answer: Yes! Doctors, called neurologists, put a cap on your head like this one and measure the electrical energy in your brain. The electrodes on your head give information to a computer. It doesn't hurt at all. The doctor can see how well your brain focuses and responds to visual and auditory input. When you do S'cool Moves, the energy in your brain changes to help you learn better.

Job: FOCUS LEADER

Goes with Minute Moves for Focus Poster

Choose one activity

Chair Lifts   OR   **Mirror Me Moves**

1. Rapid Automatic Naming (RAN) activities can be very frustrating for students with cognitive challenges and extremely slow processing speeds. The RAN portions of these activities are best used with children who have processing speeds slower than expected and are able to improve with practice (bottom quarter readers, for instance).

2. RAN speeds are often tested during psychometric evaluations from a psychologist. The score on these tests are overlooked most of the time during parent/team meetings. Be sure to notice RAN speeds as this is related to reading fluency and the child's ability to quickly process information.

3. Often neurodiverse children process auditory and visual information at different speeds than children who don't have RAN speed issues. Allow time for children with slow RAN speeds to grasp concepts and respond.

4. When asking for oral responses, invite learners to write them down first or share with a partner initially to provide more time to respond and increase participation.

5. Any of the Transition Tune-Ups can be used during, well...transitions! This is a great way to refocus after changing from one activity to the next.

General Instructions

These activities all work to improve Rapid Automatic Naming (RAN) along with vision, and motor skills. Each page contains one activitiy for vision/motor skills and another
activity to improve RAN speed. RAN speed is related to reading fluency and brain processing speed. There is a large body of research tying RAN speed to reading fluency but not a lot of information about how to improve RAN speed, so I took it upon myself to create activities to help my reading students improve their RAN speeds knowing that the way the brain gets better at something is to do it more often.

You can add music to some of the motor activities but only after students are really comfortable with them. Adele's Rolling in the Deep is fantastic with Color Taps. We oftendo this one to music during my workshops. Super fun!

Butterfly 8s

Trace in the direction of the arrows ten times with your right hand, left hand, and both hands.
Follow with your eyes, try not to move your head. Keep card at midline of body.

In a quiet voice, read the letters as fast as you can without stopping at the end of the line.

Dots Galore

● pat on desk or lap with right hand   ○ pat on desk or lap with hands crossed at wrists

● pat on desk or lap with left hand   ● pat on desk or lap with both hands

Challenge Directions: pat hands on desk or lap while tapping feet on floor at the same time. Follow the same directions as before but add your feet!

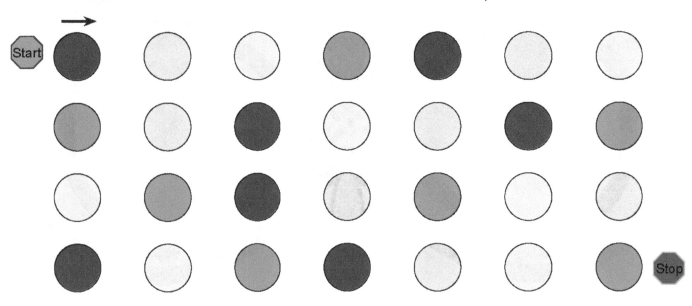

In a quiet voice, read the colored dots as fast as you can without stopping at the end of the line. You can rotate the card for variety.

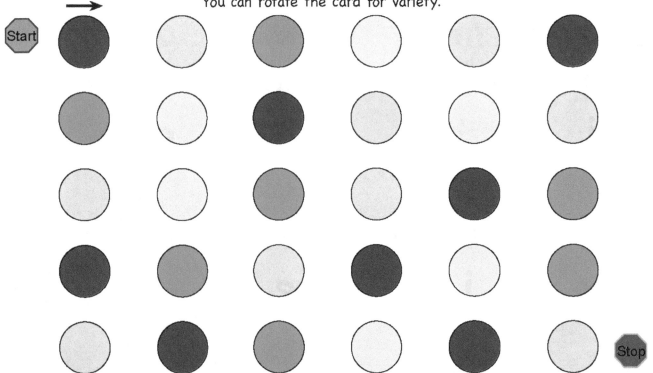

Finger Flex

Use your fingertips. Tap the correct finger on the table top. Do each row without pausing or stopping.
Use only your right hand if the numbers are red. Use only your left hand if the numbers are blue.

Start

1 2 3 4 5	5 4 3 2 1	1 2 3 4 5	5 4 3 2 1
1 2 3 4 5	5 4 3 2 1	1 2 3 4 5	5 4 3 2 1
1 2 3 4	3 1 2 3	4 3 5 4	1 3 2 4
1 2 3 4	3 1 5 4	3 4 5 2	1 1 2 4
5 2 3 1	4 2 1 3	1 3 2 4 2	5 2 4 5 4
2 4 2 5	4 2 1 5	1 2 3 4 2	2 3 1 5 5
1 1 5 5	1 4 1 5	2 4 3 5 2	2 5 1 2 3
5 5 1 1	5 4 1 5	4 2 3 1 4	5 2 4 4 3

Stop

Blue numbers: use your left hand. 5 4 3 2 1 L   Red numbers: use your right hand. 1 2 3 4 5 R

In a quiet voice, read the numbers as fast as you can without stopping at the end of the line.

Start

1	5	4	9	3	7
6	2	10	8	2	6
4	10	1	3	8	5
7	1	7	9	2	4
8	3	5	10	6	9

Stop

Line It Up

Do this activity seated or standing. Raise your arms for upper marks and tap your feet for lower marks. Pat on desk with right or left hand based on where the mark is situated on the line. Mark to the right means to pat with the right hand. Mark to the left means to pat with the left hand. Two marks means to use both hands.

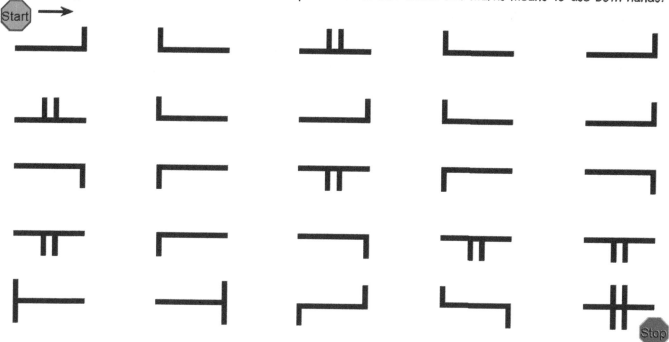

In a quiet voice, name the shapes as fast as you can without stopping at the end of the line.

● circle   ○ oval   ▭ rectangle   ‖ parallel

▲ triangle   ■ square   ◆ rhombus   ⊥ perpendicular

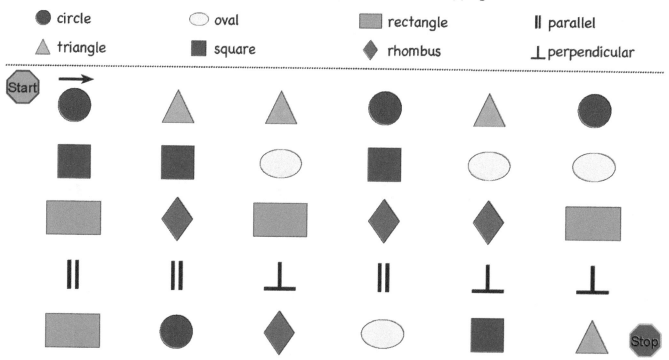

Color Taps

Use the right, left, or both hands depending on the letter within the rectangle.

- ■ tap on desk with heel of hand
- ■ tap on desk with side of hand
- ■ tap on opposite elbow with hand indicated
- □ tap on desk with full hand, palm down
- ■ tap on desk with full hand, palm up
- ■ tap on opposite shoulder with hand indicated

Start →

B	B	B	B	R	R	L	L
B	B	B	B	R	R	L	L
R	B	L	B	R	B	L	B
B	B	B	B	R	R	L	L

Stop

This is fun, but tricky! In a quiet voice, name the color of each word as fast as you can without stopping at the end of the line. Remember, don't say the word; instead, name the color.

Start →

Green	Red	Green	Blue	Yellow	Yellow
Blue	Yellow	Red	Blue	Red	Green
Green	Red	Blue	Green	Blue	Red
Green	Blue	Yellow	Red	Green	Blue
Yellow	Blue	Red	Blue	Green	Yellow
Green	Red	Green	Yellow	Blue	Green

Stop

QUICK TIPS

1. At S'cool Moves, we like to call these next set of activities Brain Boosters because they really challenge the executive functioning part of the brain. Yes, some of these activities can be really difficult! Not to worry. As long as students feel safe to take risks and are having fun, they'll lean into the challenge and feel like a su per hero when they accomplish the activities.

2. You can modify any of these activities and make them easier by not having students use the mat portion in the upper half section of the page.

3. The Brain Boost activities have been used in senior care facilities with good results. They aren't just for kids. Adults benefit from doing them as well.

4. If you have students who are color blind, some of the activities won't work well, but you can write an "r" for red inside the red dot or a "b" for blue inside the blue dot.

5. Once students can do the activities with relative confidence, work on doing the moves in a steady, rhythmic, patterned manner.

General Instructions

The Wednesday Warm-Ups are designed to improve tracking, figure-ground, bilateral integration, and executive functioning. Every activity has a "mat" at the top of the page and a "card" at the bottom of the page. In each activity, the learner will move from the bottom to the top of the page.

Quadrant Taps
Red dot means use right fist, finger, or tapping stick. Blue dot means use left fist, finger, or tapping stick. Bump with fist, tap with finger, or tap with tapping stick into the corresponding quadrant on the upper mat, moving across card from left to right.

Fast Track
Bump with fist, tap with finger, or tap with tapping sticks into the top mat. Say aloud the color on the first rectangle on the bottom card. Next find the corresponding color in the top mat. Move from left to right across the card. Alternate from left to right with each colored rectangle in a rhythmic pattern.

Brain Benders
Bump with fist, tap with finger, or tap with tapping sticks into the top mat. Look at the location of the dot on the bottom card. Next find the corresponding location in the top mat. Move from left to right across the card. Use the right or left sides of the body
depending on the color of the dot.

Brain Benders Level Up
The instructions are the same as Brain Benders only the locations are now mixed up and uses the entire mat at the same time. This activity is truly a brain bender!

Direction Dash
Bump with fist, tap with finger, or tap with tapping sticks into the top mat. Say or do the first movement on the card. Match the corresponding location on the mat. When a body part is pictured, tap on the body part. Move from left to right on the card until all moves have been completed. Alternate between the right and left sides of the body with each move.

Quadrant Taps

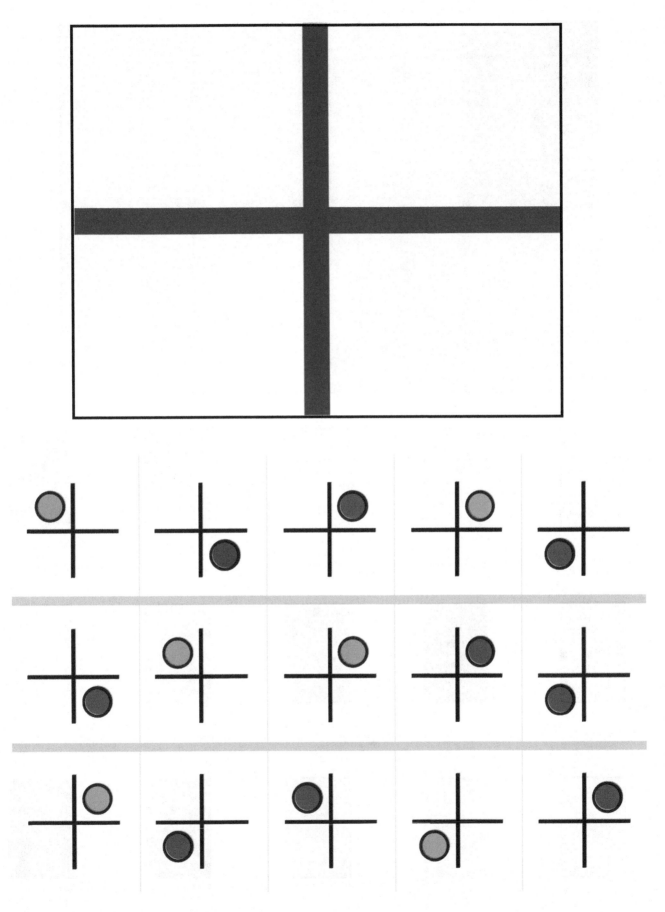

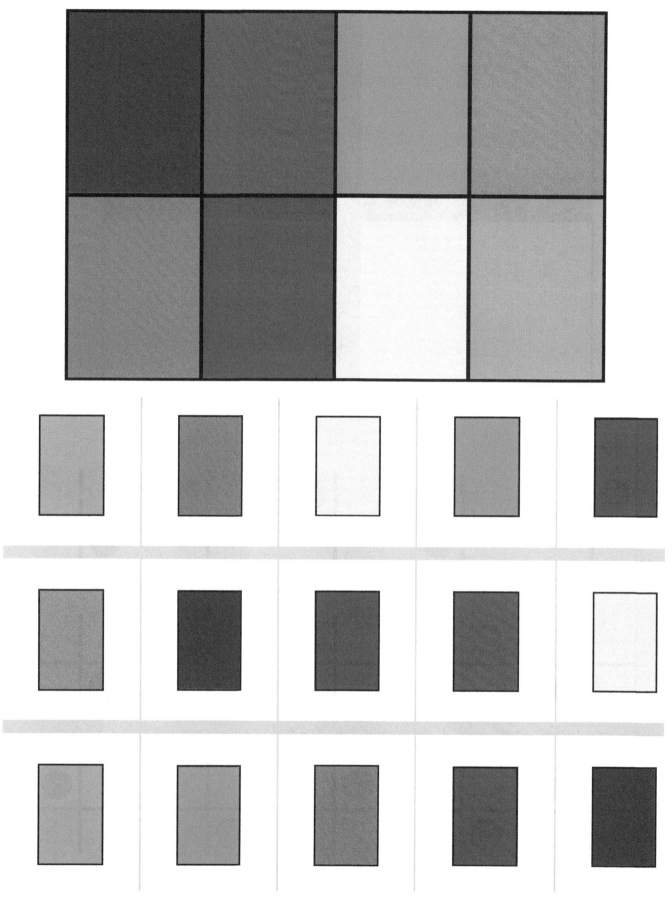

Brain Benders

Top Half

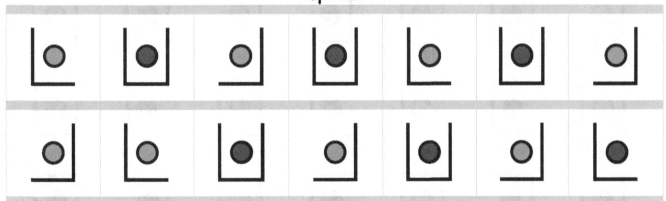

Bottom Half

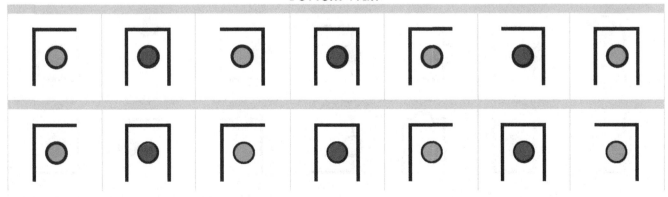

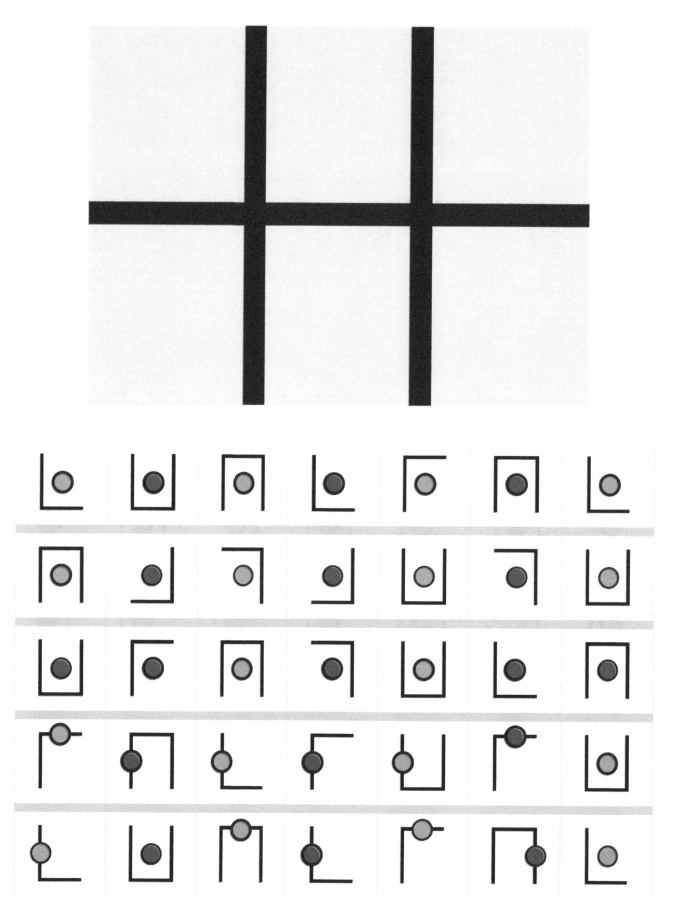

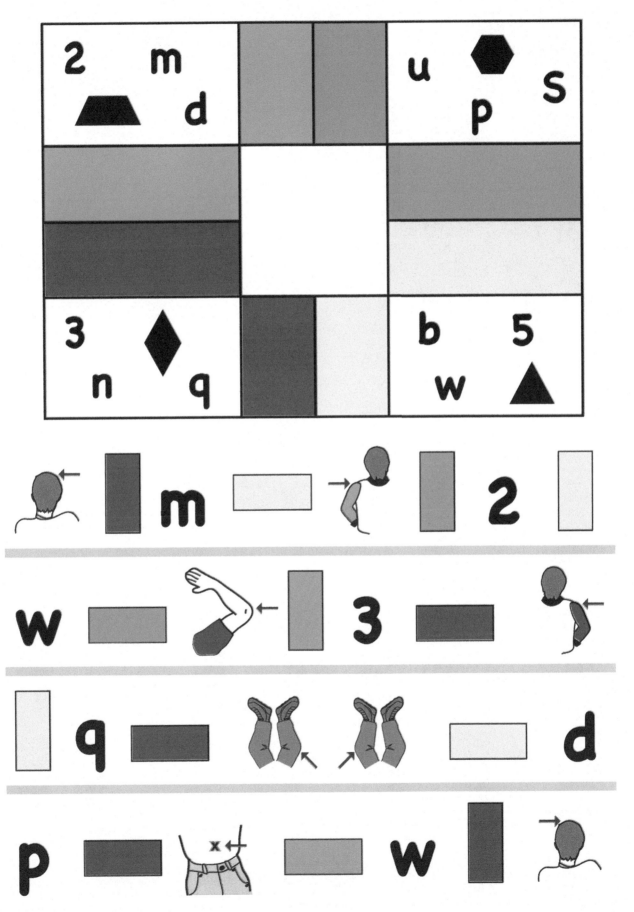

THURSDAY
THINKABLES

QUICK
TIPS

1. Adding movement to academics is one of the fastest way to increase retention of numbers, words, or concepts. You can project any of the activities in this book with a document camera or smart board. If you are working individually with a student, use sheet protectors to cover the page and write in think boxes with dry erase markers. Think boxes are what I call the blank rectangle boxes over the moves.

2. When students do moves without adding a cognitive element, they may not get the biggest bang for their cognitive buck. Having to think and move at the same time is what we do all day long. The more we practice moving and thinking, the better we get at it.

3. Have students learn the moves first before adding think boxes to the moves. Getting comfortable with the moves is important so there isn't too much stress trying to both moves and think boxes at the same time.

4. If you can't do the moves yourself, not to worry! Students love to show you how to do these activities. I often invite students to show me how to do the moves.

5. Once students can do the activities with relative confidence, work on doing the moves in a steady, rhythmic, patterned manner. You can add fun music with a steady beat.

General Instructions

1. Learn the activity first before doing the activity with the think boxes.

2. After the activity is easily done, write any letters, numbers, or words students are learning into the think boxes. Say the words while doing the associated movement.

3. All the activities in this section are color coded. Anything in red always means use the right side of the body. Blue means use the left side of the body. Green means use both sides of the body.

4. If you have taken a S'cool Moves course and are familiar with the Bop-Bink-Bounce approach to activities, you can extend the basic directions to include bopping with right and left fists, binking with red and blue tapping sticks, or bouncing red and blue racquetballs.

Individual Activity Instructions Requiring No Tools:

Figure 8s Activity: Write words in think boxes. Point to the contents of the think boxes, (alternate between using the right and left sides of the body) and say what's in the boxes while tracing the Figure 8.

Arrow Moves Activity: Move right, left, or both arms in the direction of the arrow while saying the contents of think boxes.

Press the Desk Activity: Press right, left, or both hands into the desk while saying contents of think boxes.

Focus Feet Activity: Press right, left, or both feet into the floor while saying contents of think boxes.

Hands and Feet Challenge Activity: Press hands and/or feet into the desk or floor while saying contents of think boxes.

Word Ping-Pong Activity: Write numbers or words in think boxes. Partners take turns reading content in think boxes. The first person reads the red think boxes and the second person reads the blue think boxes. This can be done with two groups as well.

With Tools:

When using red and blue tapping sticks or red and blue raquetballs, alternate based on the colors in each activity. For the color green, use both tapping sticks or both balls.

Figure 8 Thinkable Activity

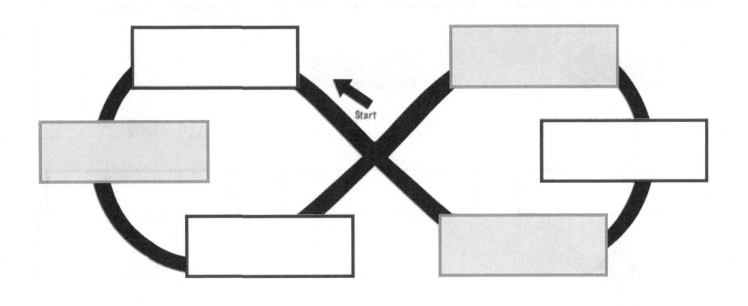

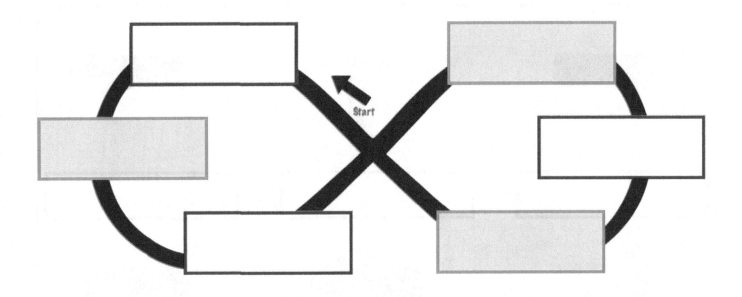

Arrow Moves Thinkable Activity

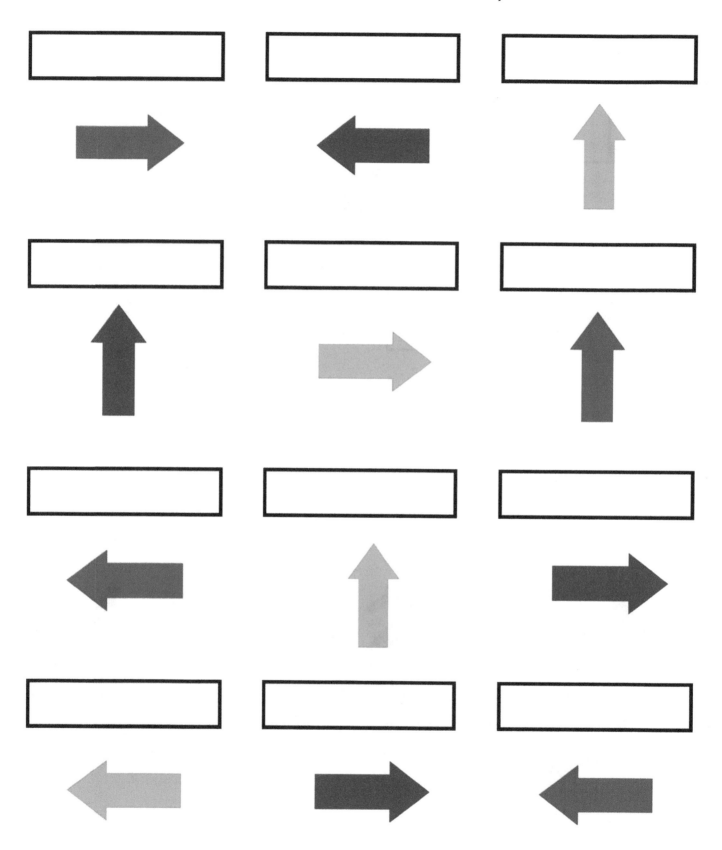

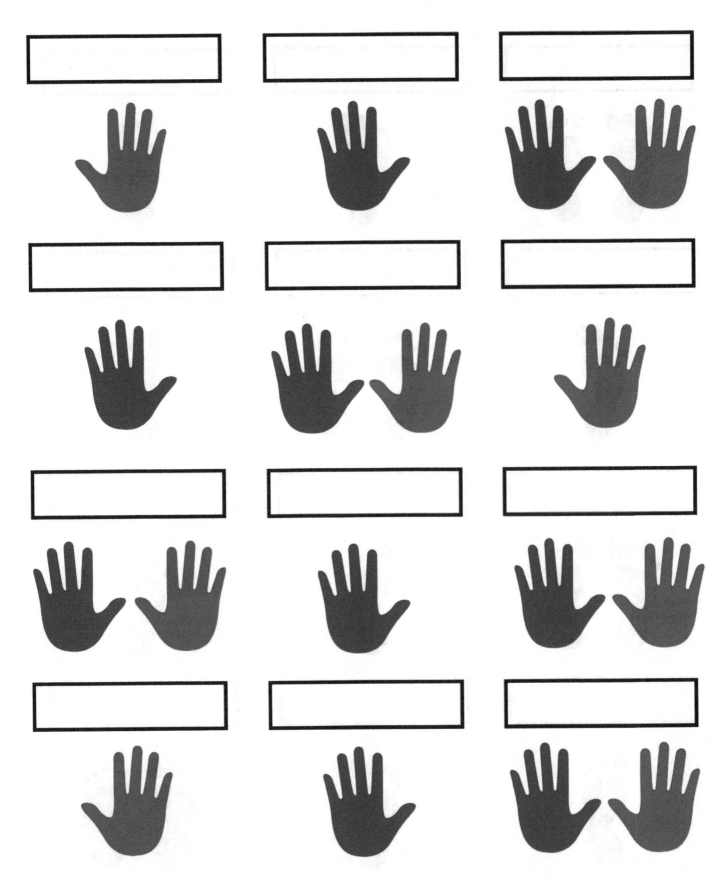

Focus Feet Thinkable Activity

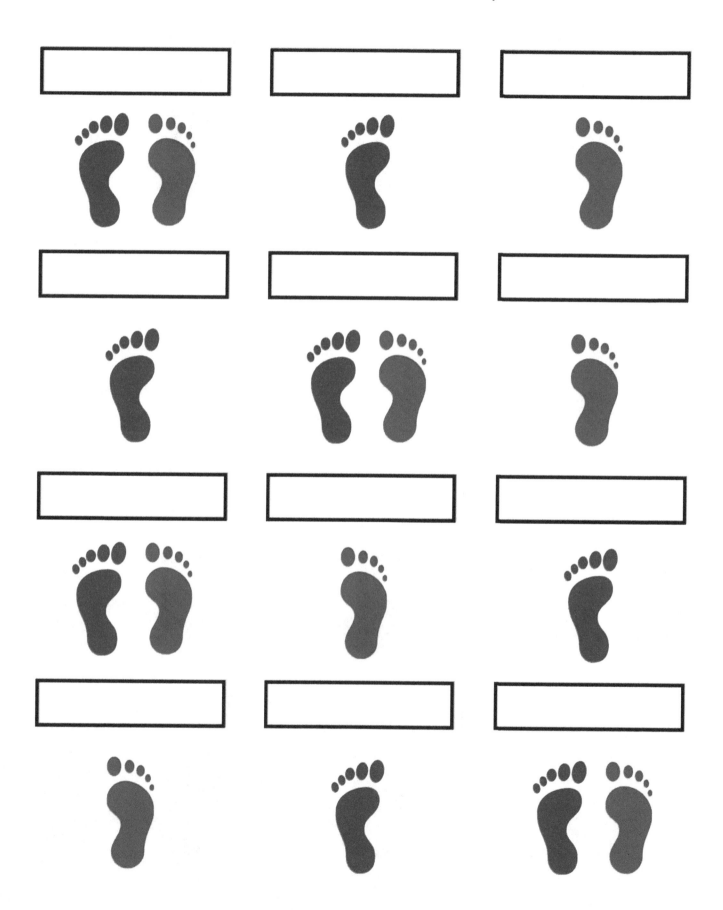

Hands and Feet Thinkable Activity

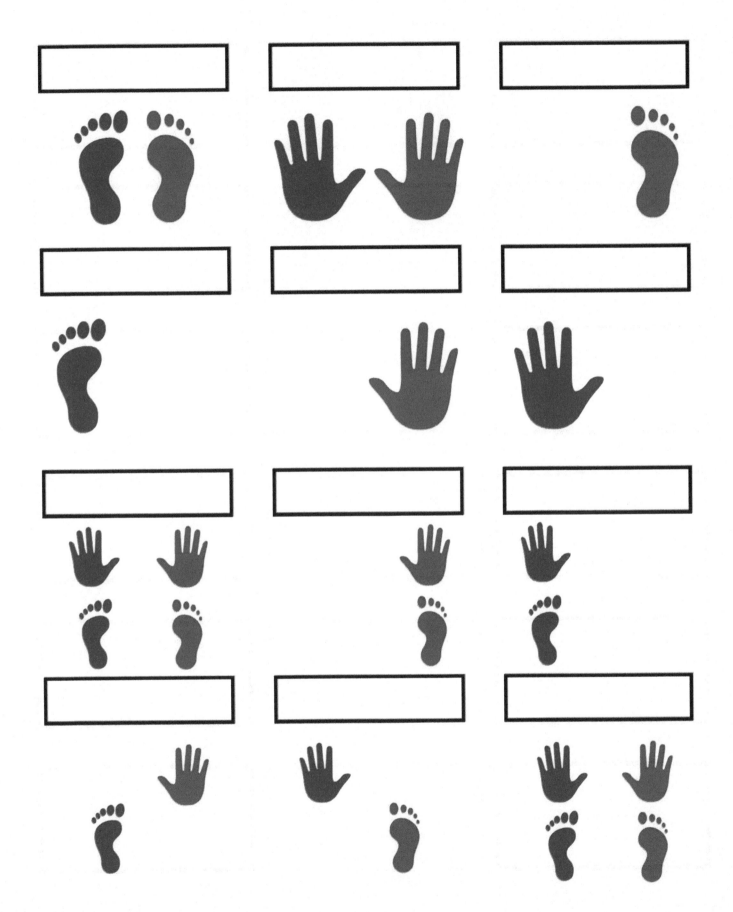

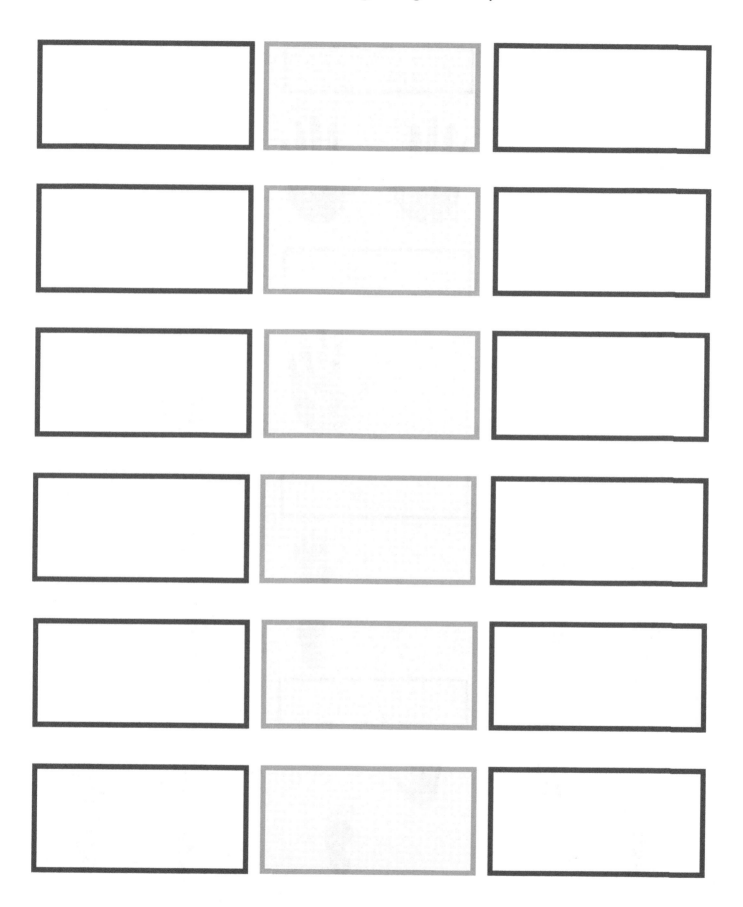

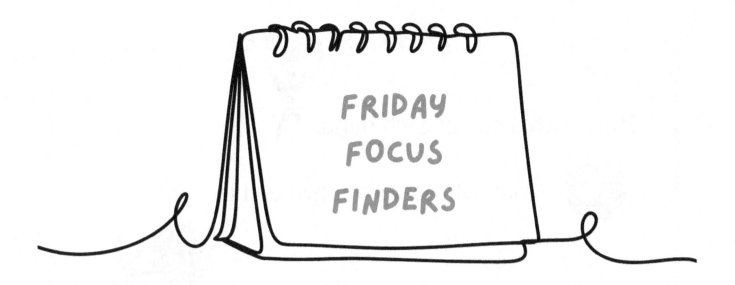

FRIDAY
FOCUS
FINDERS

QUICK
TIPS

1. Some of these activities are designed to use with red and blue racquetballs, however if no balls are available, use right and left fists, right and left index fingers, palms (press into wall/desk, raise arms (like asking a question), or stomp right or left foot.

2. If you want to tap on the shapes with unsharpened pencils, put red and blue dots on the erasers of pencils and now you have tapping sticks. You can purchase read and blue tapping sticks at our website.

3. You can also put red and blue stickers on hands to help with right and left.

4. Activities with grids on the floor can be modified with grids being taped on a wall or desk.

5. Be creative. The colored shapes can stand for anything movement that you'd like to do.

D●ts Sp●ts

Start with a ball in each hand.

 Red D●t means bounce ball in right hand.

Blue D●t means bounce ball in left hand.

 Yellow D●t means hold both balls waist high and pause for two seconds.

 Green D●t means bounce both balls.

 Stand shoulder to shoulder next to each other facing poster. Bounce balls in sync with partners.

Everyone must call out each move in unison. For example:

"right"   "left"   "both"   "pause"

Dots Spots

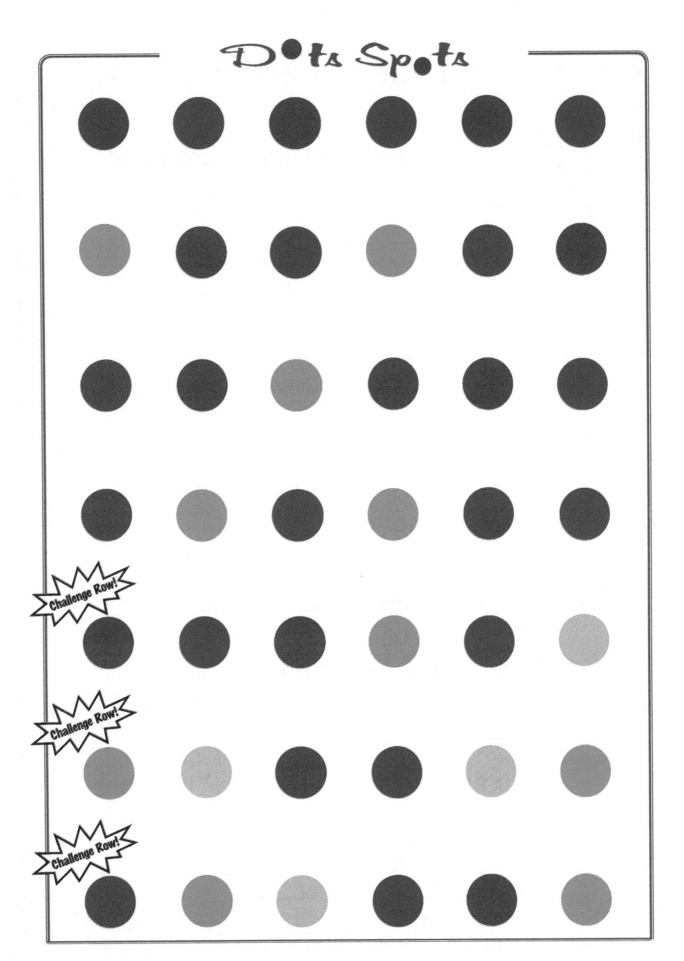

Triangle Trap

 = bounce ball with right hand

 = bounce ball with left hand

 = bounce balls with both hands

 = pause, hold balls still for 2 seconds

 = inverted triangle means go back 2 triangles and follow direction for that triangle. Pick up where you left off.

Call out all directions aloud

"right"   "left"   "both"   "pause"

Triangle Trap

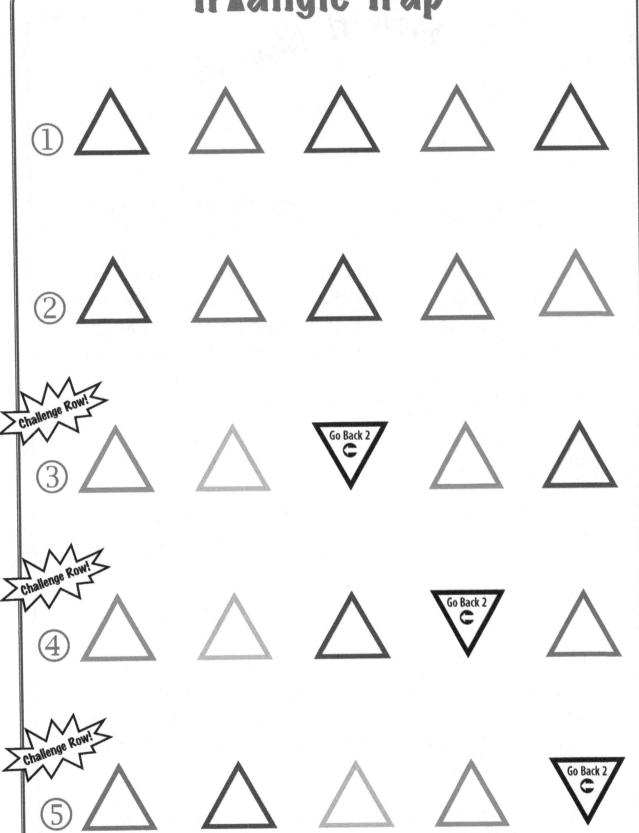

① △ △ △ △ △

② △ △ △ △ △

Challenge Row!

③ △ △ ▽ Go Back 2 △ △

Challenge Row!

④ △ △ △ ▽ Go Back 2 △

Challenge Row!

⑤ △ △ △ △ ▽ Go Back 2

Move it! Move It!

C C S P P   C C S P P

C = Pull arms back, point elbows to rear. Cross arms in front of body and punch straight out with fist and right arm while crossing right leg over left leg at the same time. Return to starting position. Then pull back both arms and punch out left fist crossing in front of body while crossing left leg over right.

P S P S   P S P S

S = Step right foot to the right. Slide left foot over to meet right foot. Clap. Do same with left leg.

C P P C   C P P C

P = Punch right arm straight out with fist while kicking straight out with right leg, karate style with a twist of the body. Reverse sides. Turn body quarter turn as you kick out. Do two times alternating on each side.

S S P P C   S S P P C

Move it! Move It!

C C S S	S C C S
P S P S	C S C S
C P P C	C P S C

Challenge Row!

S S P P C	S P P S C

Challenge Row!

P P C S P	C S P P C

Challenge Row!

C S P S P	P C P P S

Dynamic Directionals

RED Arrow = Bounce ↓ or toss ↑ ball in right hand in direction of arrow.

BLUE Arrow = Bounce ↓ or toss ↑ ball in left hand in direction of arrow.

GREEN Arrow = Bounce ↓ or toss ↑ both balls in direction of arrow.

BLACK Arrow = Each arrow equals a right then left bounce in direction of arrow.

Say each direction out loud as you follow along.

Keep legs shoulder width apart.

Dynam↑c D↑rect↑ona↳s

① ← → ← →

② ↑ ↑ ↑ ↑

③ → ← ↑ ↓

Challenge Row!

④ → ↓ ↑ ←

Challenge Row!

⑤ ← ↓ ↑ →

C●rner ⬜uandary

Make grid on floor with masking tape.
Stand with grid in front of you.

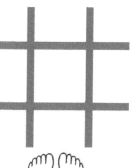

Direction One—Jump

The ● marks which section to jump into
with both feet.

Practice until you can jump smoothly from one section to
the next without pausing between jumps.

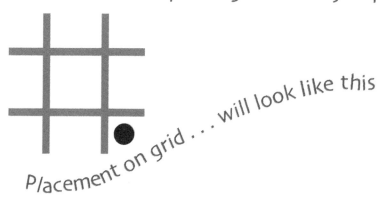

Placement on grid . . . will look like this

Direction Two— Tap

Stand in the middle square. Using right toe,
tap into each section as quickly as you can,
without pausing or moving left foot.
Repeat using left toe.

Direction Three—Twist

Stand in the middle. Remain facing front
with feet firmly planted in center square.
Rotate upper body and bounce ball into
appropriate section.

Corner Quandary

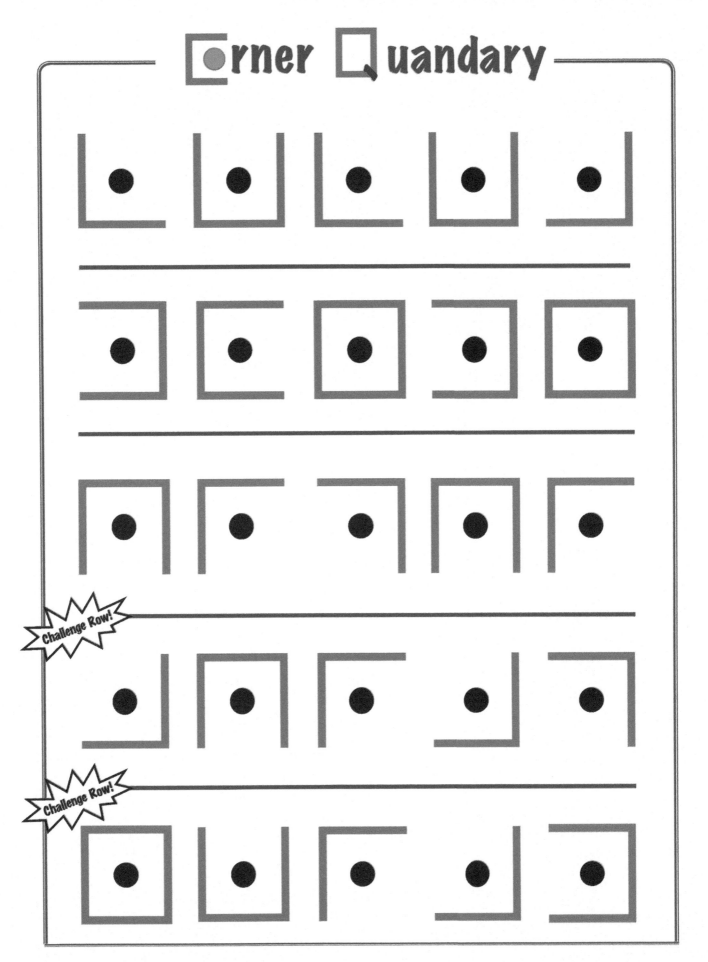

1. Twister Puzzle Card activities work on body awareness, a key factor in a student's ability to focus. If you don't know where your body is in space, it's hard to stay focused and regulated.

2. Interoception plays a key role in being able to complete these body puzzles. If you're unfamiliar with the interoceptive sense, see my interview with Kelly Mahler on my YouTube channel, @dwschoolmoves.

3. You can make bigger posters (11 x 17) so students can place them on the floor and literally sit on the poster and do their moves.

4. In the S'cool Moves course, we have these puzzles available in various formats so students can play memory match games, cut them out and make their own patterns, and so forth. If you haven't taken a course, consider doing so to learn more about this activity and all the other ones in this book.

5. Have students do the move on the card and count to eight. Stand back up and do the next move. By counting and standing back up, this provides some rhythmic and organizational aspects to the activity. It becomes less chaotic!

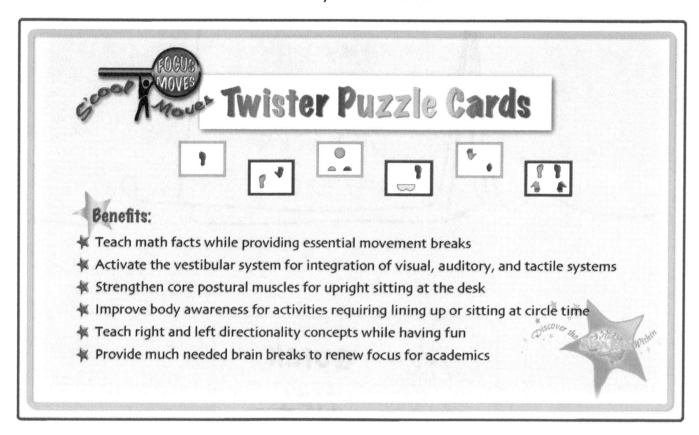

Twister Puzzle Cards

Benefits:

★ Teach math facts while providing essential movement breaks

★ Activate the vestibular system for integration of visual, auditory, and tactile systems

★ Strengthen core postural muscles for upright sitting at the desk

★ Improve body awareness for activities requiring lining up or sitting at circle time

★ Teach right and left directionality concepts while having fun

★ Provide much needed brain breaks to renew focus for academics

Twister Puzzles

Activity Directions

Twister Puzzles are also referred to as Balance Puzzles. They support the development of midline skills, body awareness, directionality, core strengthening, vestibular activation, balance, spatial skills, and math concepts.

The cards are numbered from one to ten on the front sides of the cards and eleven to twenty on the back sides of the cards. Puzzles for cards one through ten are easier to perform than for cards eleven through twenty.

Students perform each numbered movement. For young children, the use of the appropriate right or left limb is not essential.

The shapes represent body parts that are touching the floor. They translate as follows:

Head

Seat

Feet

Hands

Knees
(feet off floor)

Elbows
(hands off floor)

Remember! Only the body part that is pictured should be touching the floor. All other body parts need to be off the floor.

When children are able to perform the movements easily, have them pay attention to the picture and use the appropriate right or left limb of the body.

Adding Academics

The cards are numbered for ease of adding math concepts to the game. For instance, you can say, "All children with even numbers come up front and perform your patterns." "All children with odd numbers come up front and perform your patterns." "Find a partner whose number on their card is equal to 6 when added to your card." "Will children with card numbers two and four please come to the front. If we add two and four together, who has the card that is the answer to our equation?" "Would the students holding cards two, five, and eight come to the front. Everyone please read the number that two, five, and eight create when we put them together (two hundred fifty eight)". Use your math imagination to provide movement breaks, refresh the brain, and teach some math while you are at it!

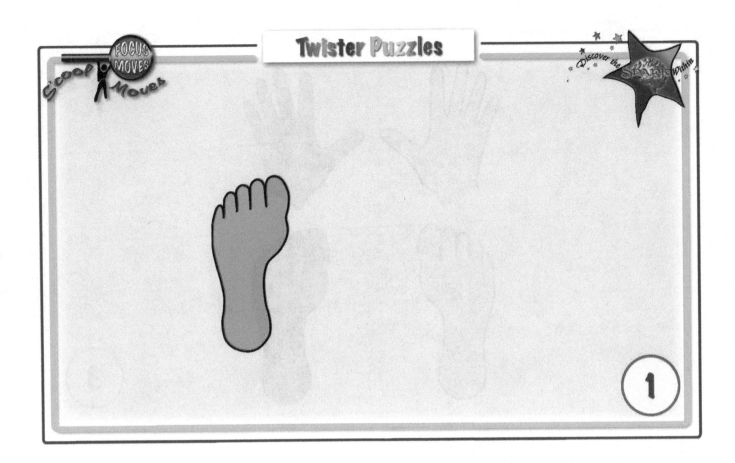

Twister Puzzles

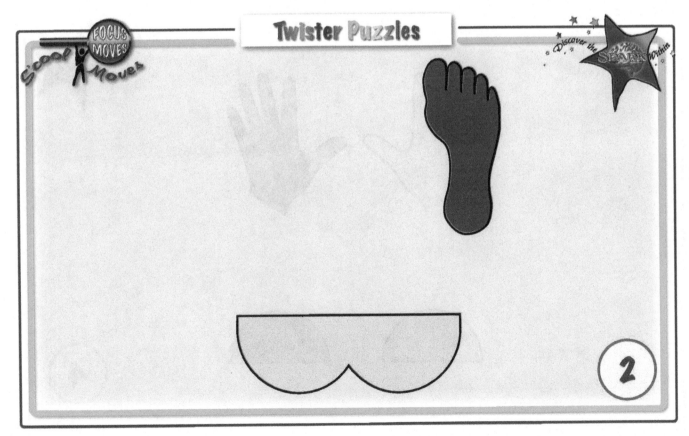

Regulated Learners in Minutes a Day

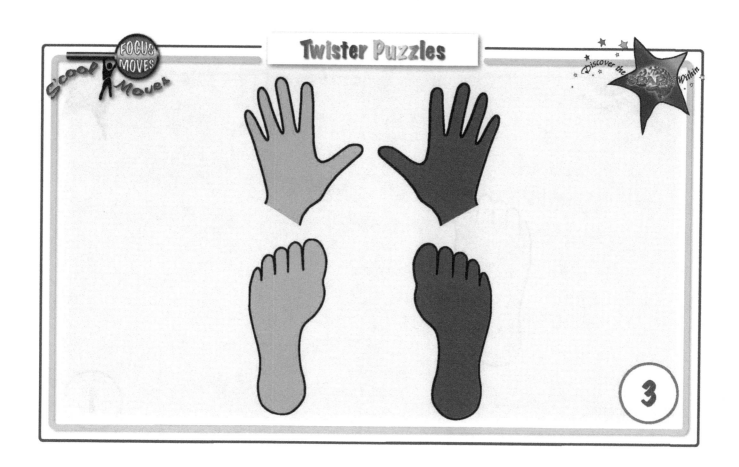

Twister Puzzles

3

Twister Puzzles

4

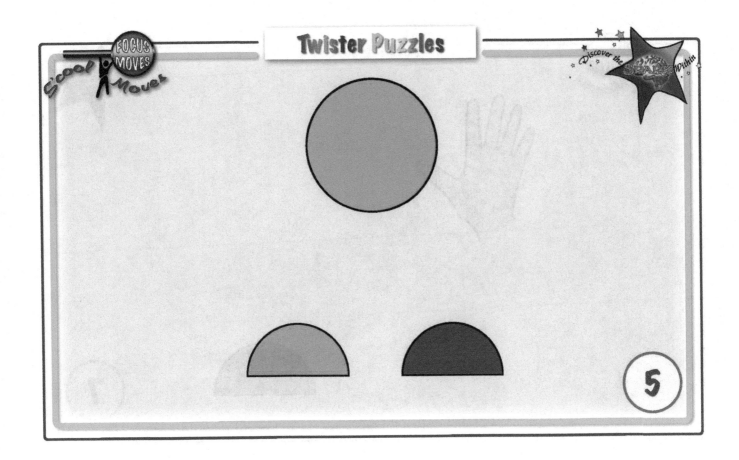

Twister Puzzles

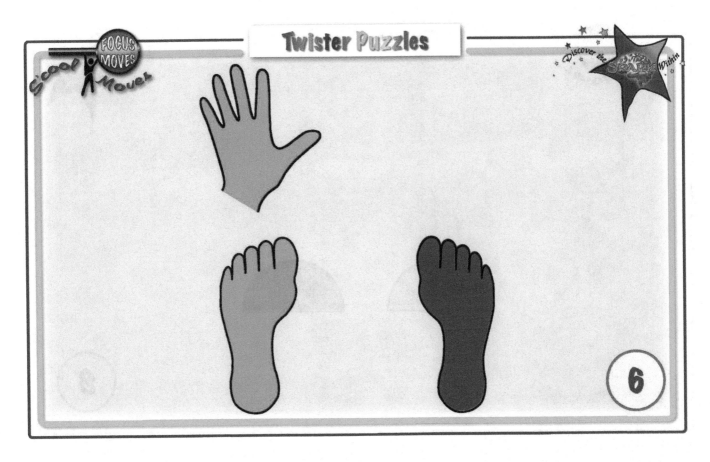

Twister Puzzles

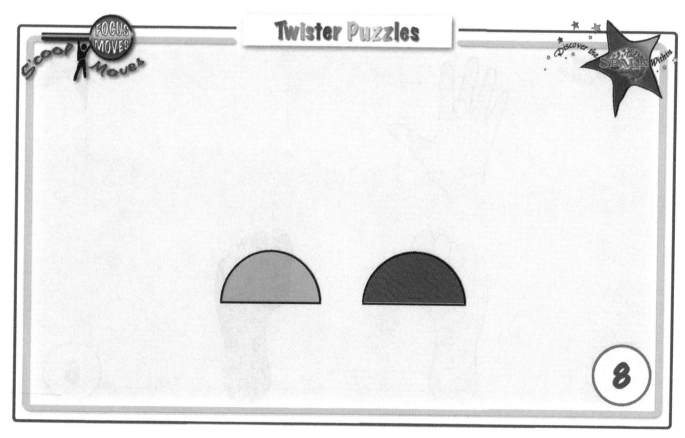

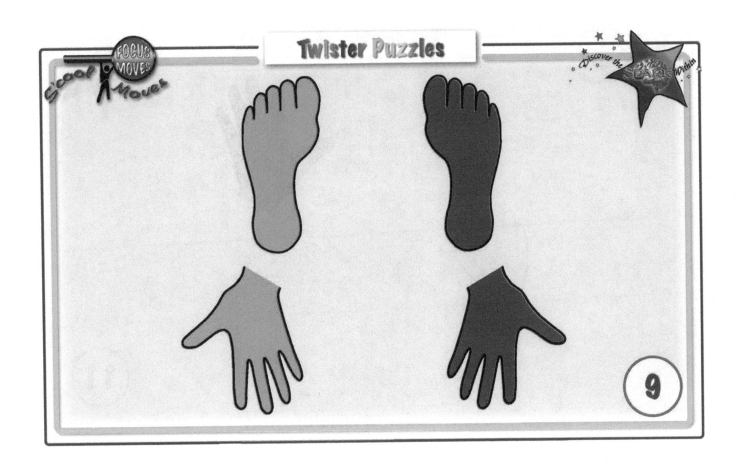

9

Twister Puzzles

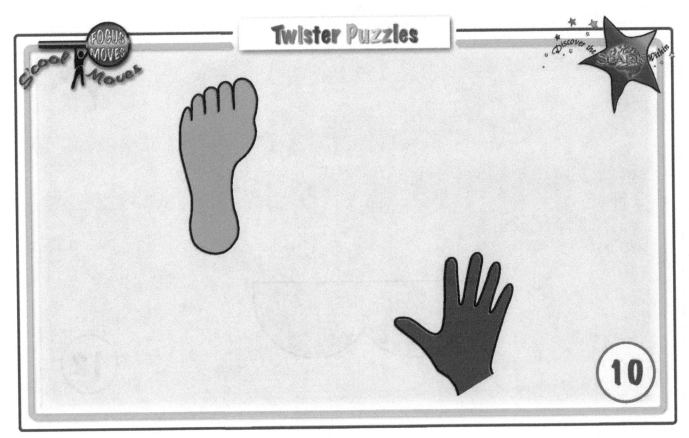

10

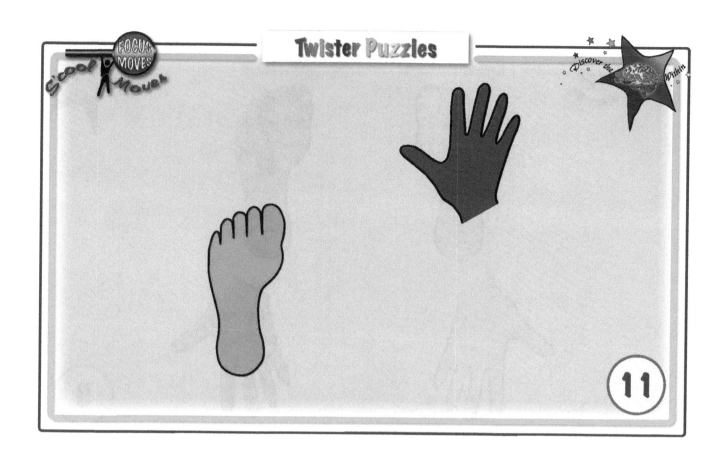

Twister Puzzles

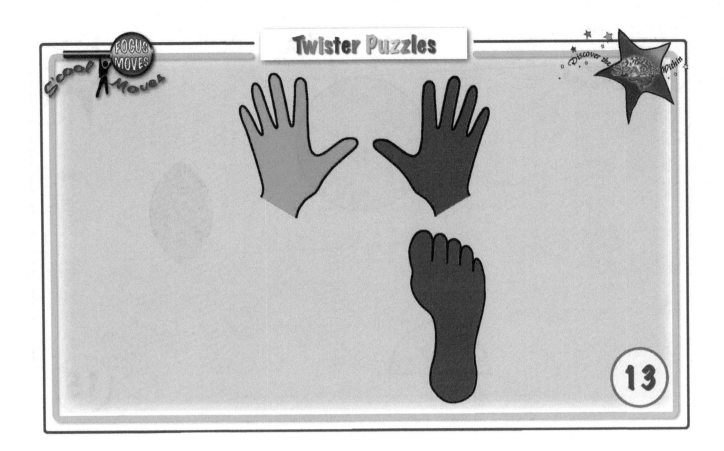

Twister Puzzles

Regulated Learners in Minutes a Day

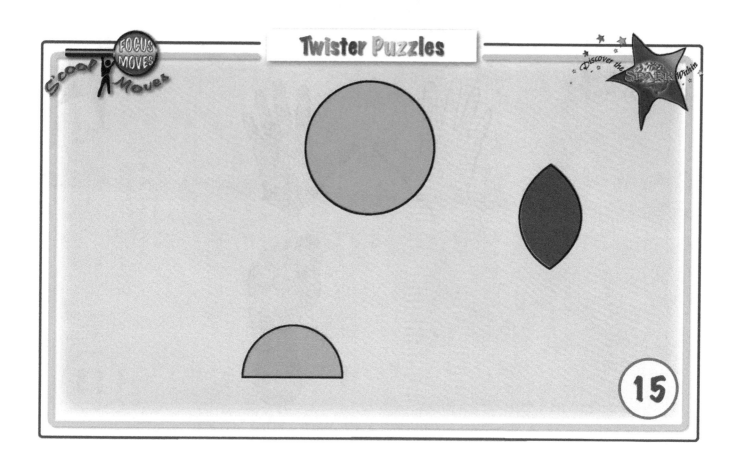

15

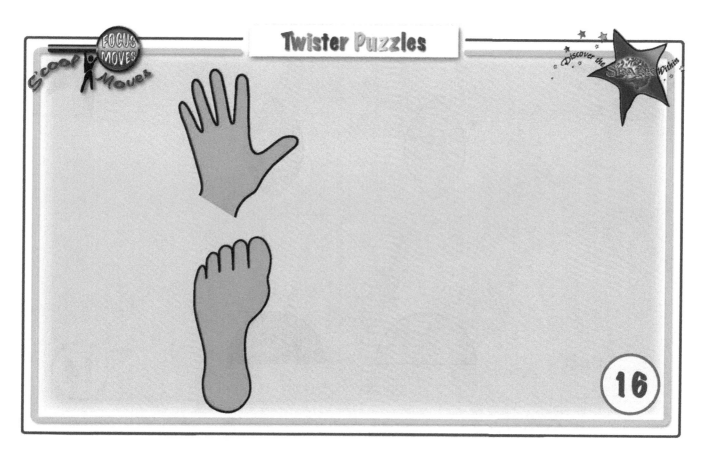

16

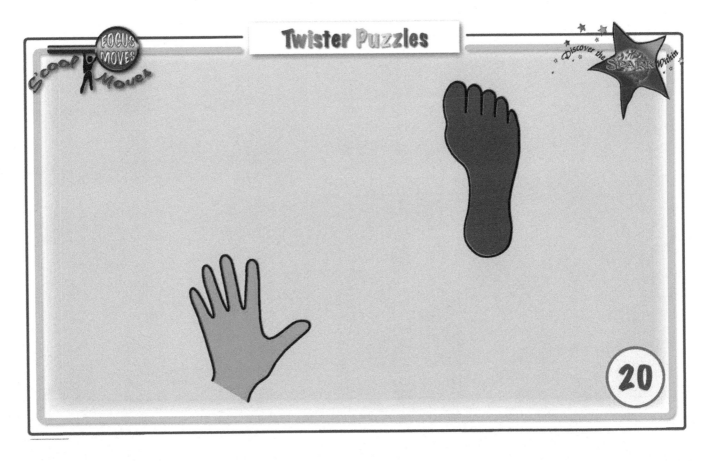

About the Author
Debra Em Wilson

I'm the Founder of S'cool Moves and a graduate from the University of Southern Queensland Professional Studies Program. My doctoral dissertation uncovered attributes of successful collaboration between occupational therapists and general education teachers working together in the classroom environment.

I'm a reading specialist and hold teaching credentials in biology, physical education, multiple subjects, and reading and language specialist. I've taught at the college, high school, and elementary levels.

I consult with districts, focusing on collaboration between support staff and teachers using neurodevelopmental movement to help with focus, regulation, and engagement. For over twenty-five years, my workshops have provided evidence-based strategies to support all students in the classroom.

I'm also the author of numerous books and instructional materials integrating neuroscience and neurodevelopmental activities into academics. My latest additions are *The Polyvagal Path to Joyful Learning: Transforming Classrooms One Nervous System at a Time* and *The Resilient Learner's Backpack: Mind-Body Activities for Focus, Regulation, and Engagement.*

My experience as the mother of a child with a constellation of challenges enhances my understanding of children who learn differently and have a difficult time fitting in with their peers. My daughter is pictured on the cover of this book. I'm also the mother of an artistic son who did the illustrations for my latest books (bribed daily with Jersey Mikes sub sandwiches).

When I'm not teaching, writing, or creating more materials, I enjoy swimming, biking, and hiking in beautiful Oro Valley, AZ.

Don't hesitate to reach out to me at info@schoolmoves.com if you have something you'd love to share or have a question for me. This book is a supplement for the S'cool Moves course. Consider taking a course to learn more. Visit www.schoolmoves.com to get more information about our on-demand courses, online blended team trainings, or on-site professional development.